Way Out in the Centre

Way Out in the Centre

Dannie Abse

Hutchinson
London Melbourne Sydney Auckland Johannesburg

Hutchinson & Co. (Publishers) Ltd

An imprint of the Hutchinson Publishing Group

3 Fitzroy Square, London W1P 6JD

Hutchinson Group (Australia) Pty Ltd
30–32 Cremorne Street, Richmond South, Victoria 3121
PO Box 151, Broadway, New South Wales 2007

Hutchinson Group (NZ) Ltd
32–34 View Road, PO Box 40–086, Glenfield, Auckland 10

Hutchinson Group (SA) (Pty) Ltd
POX Box 337, Bergvlei 2012, South Africa

First published 1981
© Dannie Abse 1981

Set in VIP Bembo by D. P. Media Ltd, Hitchin, Hertfordshire

Printed in Great Britain by The Anchor Press Ltd
and bound by Wm Brendon & Son Ltd
both of Tiptree, Essex

British Library CIP data

Abse, Dannie
  Way out in the centre.
  I. Title
  821'.9'14

ISBN 0 09 144850 6 cased
      0 09 144851 4 paper

Some of these poems were first published in: *Ambit,
The American Poetry Review, Canto, Encounter, The
Iowa Review, The Irish Press, The Jewish Chronicle
Literary Supplement, London Magazine, Madog,
Moosehead Review, Other Poetry, Outposts, Over the
Bridge* (Penguin Books), *Pick, Poems from the Medieval
World* (MTP Press), *Poetry* (Chicago), *Poetry Now*
(BBC), *The Poetry Book Society Christmas Supplement
1980, Poetry Wales, Present Tense, The Scotsman, The
Times Literary Supplement, The Vanderbilt Poetry
Review*

Joan's

Now that the evening cold is on the crocus
do you feel the ache of something missing?
Snow melts falling, a million small lights fuse

on twigs, fall to pools of darkness on the ground
while, indoors, one note's gone from the piano
– the highest. Listen to the thud of felt.

No, dear, no! Hear rather the other notes
of the right hand. Also the left background.
Their rejoicing, lamenting, candid sound.

Poems

Smile please   13
Bedtime story   14
In the gallery   16
A winter visit   18
The doctor   19
X-ray   20
Lunch and afterwards   21
Orpheus in the surgery   23
Pantomime diseases   25
Of Rabbi Yose   26
Snake   28
Of Itzig and his dog   31
Jottings   32
   Song of himself   32
   Leisure   32
   Seekers after truth   32
   Don Juan reports   33
   Freud relates his favourite joke   33
   Inspiration   33
   Transgression   34
Variations   35
   The bad boy of the North-West coast   35
   The young man and the lion   36
   Lesson in reality (1)   40
   Lesson in reality (2)   40
   A London street scene   42
Another street scene   43
The empty building at night   45
Lights in the night suburb   46
The power of prayer   48
Night village   49
Light   50
A note to Donald Davie in Tennessee   51

A sea-shell for Vernon Watkins   52
Imitations   53
One Sunday afternoon   54
In my fashion   55
Last words   56

Way Out in the Centre

Smile please
(*For Stuart Evans*)

Young, I'd startle on a dust-free hole in the air,
with electronic or magnesium flash
photograph the other side, reveal reluctant
ghosts or some rare frightful metamorphosis.

I'd catch Leda naked, her face flushed,
her body white like the swan's; or wrathful
Apollo erect and frustrated as Daphne
became less woman, more tree. There were nights

I dreamed a great light picked out momentarily
a unicorn tupping an over-exposed virgin
while other beasts, unknown to man, silently
paced from one secret world to another.

Now the invisible is dark in the blaze of noon
and I'm here and glad beneath a spired church
where over-dressed relatives throw confetti, laugh
and lurch towards a couple enlarged with love.

Older, it's scenes like this that charm me – the disguise
of comedy, blossom of a nettle, a wedding
    photograph!
And tonight I'll show you the touched-up proof
as new-minted Mr and Mrs kiss and kiss

to prove no developed metamorphosis
can be so wild or as genuine as this.

Bedtime story

Adam, the first man, my father said, perfect
like the letter A. Blessed be all alephs.
Then my clever question: were there no creatures,

father, before Adam? A long index finger
vertical as a flame to horizontal lips.
Eyes right, eyes left. Whisper of a spy:

yes, unfortunate creatures, angels botched,
badly made, born to be vagrant, born with
the usual amnesia but with little sense

and no sense of direction. They could not
deliver the simplest of messages. . . .
Now, late, I think of that flawed lineage:

of one announcing great news to the wrong Mary
– perhaps it was that unshaved derelict
at the bus station with an empty bottle, muttering –

and here's another in disguise, down at heel,
defeated face white as the salt of Sodom,
veteran among the homeward football crowd

shuffling under hoardings towards nightfall;
and this one supine, over-bearded,
sleeping on a parkbench in his excrement.

Dogs bark and bark at them. They lack pleasure.
They refrigerate the coldness of things.
They stale. They taste the age of their own mouths.

In Casualty rarely cry or grumble.
In wards die with only screens around them.
But now, father, here's *my* bedtime story:

sometimes in the last light of January,
in treeless districts of cities, in a withered
backstreet, their leader can be glimpsed from trains.

He stands motionless in long black overcoat
on spoilt snow and seems like a man again
who yet, father, will outlast the letter Z.

In the gallery

1

Outside it is snow snow
but here, under the chandelier,
there's no such thing as weather.
Right wall, a horse (not by Géricault);
left, a still life, mainly apples;
between, on the parquet floor, a box
or a coffin which is being opened.

Through a gold-framed mirror
the Director, dressed as if for mourning,
observes the bust
of an unknown lady
by an unknown sculptor
being lifted out of the straw
by a man in overalls.

2

The apples do not rot, the horse will not bolt,
the statue of the lady
cannot breathe one spot
of tissue paper on the mirror.

Her name is forgotten,
the sculptor's name is disputed,
they both have disappeared forever.
They could have been born
in the North or the South.
They have no grave anywhere.

3

Outside it is snow snow
snowing and namelessness is growing.

Yesterday four hoofmarks in the snows
rose and flew away.

They must have been four crows.
Or, maybe, three of them were crows.

A winter visit

Now she's ninety I walk through the local park
where, too cold, the usual peacocks do not screech
and neighbouring lights come on before it's dark.

Dare I affirm to her, so agèd and so frail,
that from one pale dot of peacock's sperm
spring forth all the colours of a peacock's tail?

I do. But she like the sibyl says, 'I would die';
then complains, 'This winter I'm half dead, son.'
And because it's true I want to cry.

Yet must not (although only Nothing keeps)
for I inhabit a white coat not a black
even here – and am not qualified to weep.

So I speak of small approximate things,
of how I saw, in the park, four flamingoes
standing, one-legged on ice, heads beneath wings.

The doctor

Guilty, he does not always like his patients.
But here, black fur raised, their yellow-eyed dog
mimics Cerberus, barks barks at the invisible,
so this man's politics, how he may crawl
to superiors, do not matter. A doctor must care
and the wife's on her knees in useless prayer,
the young daughter's like a waterfall.

Quiet, Cerberus! Soon enough you'll have a bone
or two. Now, coughing, the patient expects
the unjudged lie: 'Your symptoms are familiar
and benign' – someone to be cheerfully sure,
to transform tremblings, gigantic unease,
by naming like a pet some small disease
with a known aetiology, certain cure.

So the doctor will and yes he will prescribe
the usual dew from a banana leaf; poppies and
honey too; ten snowflakes or something whiter
from the bole of a tree; the clearest water
ever, melting ice from a mountain lake;
sunlight from waterfall's edge, rainbow smoke;
tears from eyelashes of the daughter.

X-ray

Some prowl sea-beds, some hurtle to a star
and, mother, some obsessed turn over every stone
or open graves to let that starlight in.
There are men who would open anything.

Harvey, the circulation of the blood,
and Freud, the circulation of our dreams,
pried honourably and honoured are
like all explorers. Men who'd open men.

And those others, mother, with diseases
like great streets named after them: Addison,
Parkinson, Hodgkin – physicians who'd arrive
fast and first on any sour death-bed scene.

I am their slowcoach colleague, half afraid,
incurious. As a boy it was so: you know how
my small hand never teased to pieces
an alarm clock or flensed a perished mouse.

And this larger hand's the same. It stretches now
out from a white sleeve to hold up, mother,
your X-ray to the glowing screen. My eyes look
but don't want to; I still don't want to know.

Lunch and afterwards

Lunch with a pathologist

My colleague knows by heart the morbid verse
of facts – the dead weight of a man's liver,
a woman's lungs, a baby's kidneys.

At lunch he recited unforgettably,
'After death, of all soft tissues the brain's
the first to vanish, the uterus the last.'

'Yes,' I said, 'at dawn I've seen silhouettes
hunched in a field against the skyline, each one
feasting, preoccupied, silent as gas.

Partial to women they've stripped women bare
and left behind only the taboo food,
the uterus, inside the skeleton.'

My colleague wiped his mouth with a napkin,
hummed, picked shredded meat from his canines,
said, 'You're a peculiar fellow, Abse.'

No reply

Why?

                                because
when I went home no one was home
because I knew I was awake
(a man asleep is a man enslaved)
I stood up walked into the hall
where I dialled the number
because of some strange ancestor
because I'm Welsh because I'm a Jew
because the audible clock's rounder
than any circle I can draw
because I've shared the particular
lunatic boredom of caged animals
because I've been touched on a scar
and felt nothing or almost nothing
because when sick I'm still a doctor
because pathologists aver
'The first organ to disappear
is the brain – the uterus the last'
because I shan't forget that ever
because I walked into the hall where
I stood next to the telephone
I thought of a number doubled it.

Orpheus in the surgery

They say the accompanying god,
when you turned abruptly to your wife,
held her fast and cried resigned, 'He has turned!'
But she, grasping nothing, whispered, '*Who?*'
How often, lost at some terminal bed,
have I recalled her question, been moved by it.

Doctor, you're fooled, that story's half untrue.
When I raised high the torch and slowly turned

I saw no one and no one spoke but me.
I daresay, far below, Ixion's wheel stopped,

sweating Sisyphus paused, shoulder to the rock,
and the forty-nine daughters of Danaus

stood still, their profiles listening. For they knew,
being accursed, my secret – why I had turned.

But above, at the eye-creasing O, the crowds,
those living silhouettes awaiting me

under the active bunting, the dignitaries,
TV crews, they did not know and asked, 'Why?'

So I lied – call it poet's gossip – not daring
to confess, as I now do, my absurd,

obscene imaginings: how I'd thought a stranger –
no god he – had sexually sipped my wife;

how she, in turn, all glue, moaned such vile
endearments, such drowsy syrups of love.

That's why I raised the torch, why in anguish,
doctor, it was I, not she, who whispered, '*Who?*'

Pantomime diseases

When the fat Prince french-kissed Sleeping Beauty
her eyelids opened wide. She heard applause,
the photographer's shout, wedding-guest laughter.
Poor girl – she married the Prince out of duty
and suffered insomnia ever after.

The lies of Once-upon-a-Time appal.
Cinderella seeing white mice grow into horses
shrank to the wall – an event so ominous
she didn't go to the Armed Forces Ball
but phoned up Alcoholics Anonymous.

Snow White suffered from profound anaemia.
The genie warned, 'Aladdin, you'll go blind,'
when that little lad gleefully rubbed his lamp.
The Babes in the Wood died of pneumonia.
D. Whittington turned back because of cramp.

Shy, in the surgery, Red Riding Hood undressed
– Dr Wolff, the fool, diagnosed Scarlet Fever
That Jill who tumbled down has wrecked her back,
that Puss-in-Boots has gout and is depressed
and one bare bear gave Goldilocks a heart attack.

When the three Darling children thought they'd fly
to Never-Never Land – the usual trip –
their pinpoint pupils betrayed addiction.
And not hooked by Captain Hook but by
that ponce, Peter Pan! All the rest is fiction.

Of Rabbi Yose

I know little except he would ponder
on the meaning of words in the Torah
till those words became more mysterious
became an astonishment and an error.

'Thou shalt grope at noonday
as the blind gropeth in darkness.'
Soon Yose's eyebrows raised
from that poetry page of curses.
Instead he stared at the adventure
of a white wall and said, 'What difference
to a blind man, noon or midnight?'

All that week, all that month
he puzzled it, '. . . as the blind gropeth . . .',
not reading it as a child would
without obstruction, nor understanding it
as a child could. He thought, too,
of his neighbour, the blind man.

Then coming home late one night
after discussing the Torah with a pupil,
or sickness with a sick man,
one suffering perhaps from the botch
of Egypt, or from emerods, or the scab,

he saw near the darkest foliage
the plumed yellow flame of a torch
moving towards him, held high in the hand
of his neighbour, the blind man.

'Neighbour,' he cried, 'why this torch
since you are blind?' The night waited
for an answer: the wind in a carob tree,
two men, one blind, both bearded, so many
shadows thrown and fleeing from the torch.

'So that others may see me, of course,'
replied the neighbour, 'and save me
from quicksand and rock, from the snake asleep,
from cactus, from thistle and from thornbush,
from the deep potholes in the roadway.'

Year after year, to pupil after pupil,
Yose told of this night-meeting,
told it as parable, told it smiling,
satisfied, with clear-seeing eyes,
and never again pondered the true
lucid meaning of the words:
'Thou shalt grope at noonday
as the blind gropeth in darkness.'

Snake

When the snake bit
Rabbi Hanina ben Dosa
while he was praying

the snake died. (Each day
is attended by surprises
or it is nothing.)

Question: was the bare-footed,
smelly Rabbi more poisonous
than the snake

or so God-adulterated
he'd become immune
to serpent poison?

Oh great-great-great-uncles,
your palms weighing air,
why are you arguing?

Listen, the snake thought
(being old and unwell
and bad-tempered as hell)

Death, where's thy sting?
In short, was just testing:
a snake's last fling.

Yes, the *so-called* snake
was dying anyway, its heart
calcified and as old as Eden.

No, that snake was A1 fit
but while hissing for fun it
clumsily bit its own tongue.

No, Hanina invented that snake;
not for his own sake but for first–
class, religious publicity.

No no, here's the key to it.
Ask: did the Rabbi, later on,
become a jumpy, timid man?

Remember, he who has been bitten
by a snake thereafter becomes
frightened of a rope. . . .

Bearded men in darkening rooms
sipping lemon tea and arguing
about the serpent till the moon

of Russia, of Latvia, Lithuania,
Poland, rose above the alien
steeples – centuries of sleep.

Now, tonight, a clean-shaven rabbi
who once studied in Vienna
says snake-venom contains

haemolysins, haemo-
coagulants, protolysins,
cytolysins and neurotoxins

and that even in Hanina
ben Dosa's day a snake was a
snake – unless, of course, it was

a penis, an unruly penis,
making a noise like one pissing
on a mound of fresh hot ashes.

Oh great-great-great-uncles
did you hear him? And are your
handbones weighing moonshine?

Of Itzig and his dog

To pray for the impossible,
says Itzig, is disgraceful.
I prefer, when I'm on my own,
when I'm only with my dog,
when I can't go out
because of the weather,
because of my shoes,
to talk very intimately to God.

       Itzig, they nag, why do that,
    what's the point of that?
    God never replies surely?

Such ignorance! Am I at the Western Wall?
Am I on spacious Mount Sinai?
Is there a thornbush in this murky room?
God may never say a word,
may never even whisper, Itzig, hullo.

But when I'm talking away
to the right and to the left,
when it's raining outside,
when there's rain on the glass,
when I say please God this
and thank God that,
then God always makes, believe me,
the dog's tail wag.

Jottings

Song of himself

Whatever was broken, rejected or lost,
he would, thrillingly amok, sing its praises
and for the length of his eye-brimming song
would feel like some strange, magnificent king,
not one broken, rejected and lost.

Leisure

They claim you're a happy man, Sisyphus,
even at the foot of the mountain.
Now thanks to the micro-chip and the Union
of Rockpushers soon such endless holidays!
What will you do, what *will* you do, Sisyphus?

Why, I'll go ski-ing of course. I'll climb
the mountain then I'll come down again.

Seekers after truth

Another climbs and climbs, mad-eyed,
far from the dancer and the lyre;
but when he looks up towards the blue
always the mountain grows higher.

Below, distant, the roaring courtiers
rise to their feet – less shocked than irate.
Salome has dropped the seventh veil
and they've discovered there are eight.

Don Juan reports

In the evening she looked like Rachel sweetly
and sweetly said, 'Make yourself feel at home.'
But in the morning she looked like Leah plainly
and I thought I'd rather feel at home at home.

Freud relates his favourite joke

While tracing the fountain to its source
walking I encountered Itzig riding.
'Where are you going?' I asked that wild-eyed rider.
'Don't ask me,' said Itzig, 'ask the horse.'

Inspiration

Above Professor Einstein's bed
a portrait of Isaac Newton.
One night Einstein bit an apple and
that portrait fell upon his head.

Transgression

When Eve held in her right hand
the forbidden apple
nothing happened.
So she took a little bite,
a cautious little bite,
and nothing happened.
The great sun shone,
the waterfall fell,
the Paradise birds continued to sing,
so she took another bite
and then another bite,
munch munch munch,
until she'd swallowed the whole damned thing.

Variations
The bad boy of the North-West coast

Before the grown-ups awake	– haaya
and the wind blows out the stars	– haaya
I'll rise and escape from home	– haaya
I'll take clubs for the salmon	– haaya
carved hooks for the halibut	– haaya
I'll paddle the great canoe	– haaya
At home they'll cry they'll miss me	– haaya
I'll hunt for big-breasted girls	– haaya
I'll give them boiled coloured sweets	– haaya
and bracelets carved of goat horn	– haaya
When I'm tall I'll bring them home	– haaya
Then all my leering uncles	– haaya
will wear their hats of spruce root	– haaya
will drum and shake their rattles	– haaya
But I'll thrash each one of them	– haaya
I'll tear off my father's head-dress	– haaya
I'll marry two girls at once	– haaya
The smaller of the darlings	– haaya
I'll dress in spotted sealskins	– haaya
and earrings of abalone shell	– haaya
the other with bigger breasts	– haaya
shan't wear anything at all	– haaya

American Indian Song

The young man and the lion
(*For Tony Whittome*)

1

Such thirst, such afternoon heat!
First it would drink then it would eat.
It trod his head into a zwart-storm tree.
                    Silently
the young man wept.

The young man who had slept
beside the zwart-storm tree and who
                    on waking
in the oven of a lion's mouth
had feigned to be dead.

The lion licked the man's two eyes.
The man felt a stick
pierce that hollow in the back
                    of his neck.
So he turned his head a little.

He looked at the lion
                    steadfastly.
The lion thought, Is he alive?
And the young man guessing that
it thought he may be alive

settled, would not stir though the stick
sharply was piercing him;
                    would not stir
till the lion who first would drink
went three hills away to drink.

Dead, thought the lion. So it went
to drink water from the water.
And the man shifted. And the man ran
                    to leave meat-
odour in the zwart-storm tree.

2

'Help!' Zig-zag he ran, open-mouthed.
'Help! Hide me in a hartebeest skin,
save me!' we heard him shout.
'The lion that drank my tears
will surely seek me out.'

Under evening miles of coloured sky
roaring and roaring the lion came
to our village. It would not cease.
The mother of the young man cried,
'Oh kill the lion, kill the beast.'

We hunters raced from the huts,
vultures settled on a wall.
One-eyed we fattened our bows
and aimed at the cheated lion.
The lion was full of arrows.

Strange thing: the lion did not fall,
would not die. What was happening?
We aimed more arrows and some hurled
assagai. Still it would not bleed.
Its soul was in another world.

'Yes,' said the rattle man who knew best.
'That lion by a sorcerer
is charmed or else it would be dead.
Give up the man you're hiding
now the sun is round as blood.'

'No!' the mouth of the mother screamed.
'Not my son, no! I shall go instead.'
And arms outstretched ran out unarmed.
Later we tossed a white-eyed girl child
to the beast. She also was not harmed.

The lion wanted only that man
whose double tears it had drunk.
Roaring it woke the stars in the sky
– they came forth brightly one by one
to watch the lion that would not die.

From the hartebeest skin we pushed him out
and the lion swallowed its roar.
Bristling with arrows, with spears,
it trod the young man, it bit him.
It drank once more his double tears.

Now free to die the lion bled
through its hide blackly. In the dark
it died where the young man lay dead
on the ground. Far from the stars,
the dead man, the dead lion.

A Bushman Legend (Katkop dialect)

Lesson in reality (1)

If you see an evil man coming towards you and feel afraid, make the sign of Shaddai, the sign of the Almighty, with your right hand and cover your face with it.

Not one man but many
wherever I looked. Here. There.
In every city, every country,

my hand flew to my falling face –
middle fingers, a three-pronged *shin*,
my thumb bent to a *dalet*,
my little finger a crooked *yod*.
The sign of Shaddai.

I grew older:
my forehead spread massively,
my frightened right eye to the right,
my frightened left eye to the left,
and the palm of my hand now too small.

T. Carmi (Hebrew)

Lesson in reality (2)

They held up a stone.
  I said, 'Stone.'
Smiling they said, 'Stone.'

40

They showed me a tree.
  I said, 'Tree.'
Smiling they said, 'Tree.'

They shed a man's blood.
  I said, 'Blood.'
Smiling they said, 'Paint.'

They shed a man's blood.
  I said, 'Blood.'
Smiling they said, 'Paint.'

Amir Gilboa (Hebrew)

A London street scene

The brown paper
that you described
rolling over

a New Jersey street
and crushed under
tyres of a car

to rise man-sized
in the same wind
down the same road

must have floated
cloud-high above
the Atlantic.

Decades it took
to descend here
in London traffic

more alive than you
to cross with care
at this zebra.

W.C.W.

Another street scene
(Outside the grocer's, Golders Green Road)

They quarrel, this black-bearded man
and his busy, almost flying wife –
she with her hands, he with proverbs.

'He who never rebukes his son,'
says the bearded man too blandly,
'leads him into delinquency.'

And she who hasn't studied nicely
such studied wisdom, now replies,
'You're a, you're a, you're a donkey.'

Three or four psychiatrists smile
as they pass the greengrocer's shop.
Again, patient, he quotes the Talmud:

'When one suggests you're a donkey
do not fret; only when two speak thus
go buy yourself a saddle.'

But she has thrown appropriate
carrots carrots at his sober head
and one sticks brightly in his beard.

Truce! You have been led into fiction.
Listen! Here comes a violin
and tunes to make a donkey dance.

The bearded man has closed his eyes.
Who's this, disguised as a beggar,
playing a violin without strings?

What music's this, its cold measure?
Who are these, dangling from lampposts,
kicking as if under water?

The empty building at night

This busy morning the ten-year-old office tower
was still unoccupied, still halfway up
to an aeroplane that pursued Heathrow,
and I went to work, frowned at the enthronement
of emptiness, was not appeased by
its compelling stories of uncurtained windows,
swarming rumours of ghost clouds, ghost sky.

Now, tonight, late, head down, hurrying home
I would ignore the dark building devoid of men
and deny again that the emptiness inside it
is part of my life, loathed by me because so;
yet I do look up, as if by ordinance, to see alas
what I knew I would: the wakeful moon too near,
untenanted, terrific on its glass.

Lights in the night suburb

1

The first perfect night of the New Year
and there is the obvious moon and here
are the lights no one foretold, springing
like oblongs to bedroom windows
across the road from each other.

2

At the third stroke it will be 9.24 p.m.
and Joanna Cash draws her right hand
first to the right and then to the left
to create the shuffling metallic
interrupted sound of pulled curtains.

At 9.25 p.m. bespectacled Isaac Parr,
the neighbour opposite in No. 26,
hands in pockets, approaches the brilliant
bare blackness of *his* bedroom window
and, somewhat lonely, peers out at lampposts.

This is London. Joanna Cash and Isaac Parr
do not know each other, never will.
Soon Isaac Parr will lurk downstairs,
switch on TV. Soon Joanna Cash
will wash her hair with the product
frequently advertised on TV.

3

Surely, earlier, one of the old gods
furtively walked through the night suburbs,
beard tilted forty-five degrees towards the moon,
saw windows light up conspiratorially
and was frightened into vanishings?

For now the street is deserted.
Not a footstep.
Lost under the furthest lamppost
a still round blob of moonlight.
Perfect night, perfect cloudless night.

The power of prayer

A kind of tune, heart in pilgrimage, yes,
    but reversed thunder as Herbert said
Herbert was right or we were April fools
last night when we beheld a sign. Behold!
    our Indian neighbour surely praying
since every house across the road was dark
except his own – his bedroom lit by volts,
no doubt, of the thunderstruck eternal.
Why else would those high surprising windows
be raging steadily with sheet lightning?

Herbert, such prayer-power! You'd not credit
    these other, raving, more ancient gods
summoned here by fervent invitation.
How they swarmed in rudely, none so rampant
    as Agni – tawny hair, all gold teeth,
long golden beard – whooping it up crazy
in that attic crackling room, his crimson
snorting horses and his dwarf golden car.
These wild, drunken fire deities! Neighbour,
we thought, oh cease praying do, for God's sake.

And just in case called the bell-mad earthly
    fire brigade whose hoses curved and hushed
so that the gods quit, disguised cleverly,
of course, as tiny butterflies of fire
    or billowing out in cloaks of smoke
and sacred steam. Now no more thunderstorms,
only black debris of last night's party.
And so we godless ones give thanks to God
for godless neighbours this April morning
and for ladders more than rainbows, Herbert.

Night village

No hare pulls a legless man screaming
into the headlights by his beard.
Driving through the night is not dreaming.

Now it's after two and we are close
to a village asleep which is no
place much. It seems to be all there is.

Here's a few small shops, their unseen glass.
Here's two great dazzling headlights
approaching selfishly. They do not pass.

For at the far corner they are thrown
nowhere. Opposite the Shell garage
closed, suddenly, they're proved to be our own.

This is the brief empty blazing High Street
connecting the one dark road coming in
to the one dark road going out.

And we accelerate, become the speed
of night. Behind us, silence resumes while,
in the mirror, the village lights recede.

No hare pulls a legless man screaming
into the headlights by his beard.
Driving through the night is not dreaming.

Light

Waking from a poorly lit dream
so fast forgetting it
that coming downstairs whistling
I forgot even forgetting.

A letter said, Poets should hold up
lamps in bad light. Why? That others
may see the corpse with placard round
its neck. I could smell gas.

And this for breakfast. The only
permitted whistling seemed to be
the victim's severed windpipe.
Now morning sky dull as ashes.

Forgive me corpse with placard round
your neck. And you, dybbuk, whistling.
Sometimes a man must close his eyes
and ears. So letter to the waste-basket.

Yet, later, rapping the table
without intent, noise in my knuckles,
I discovered the sudden gleam of dead
light from last night's dream.

Less a discovery than a recovery.
Silence and glass in a room –
glass in the window and glass
in the mirror facing that window.

A note to Donald Davie in Tennessee

Wigged gluttony never your style but will you
                                    always eschew,
barbered, the anorexia of fanaticism?
Though we would seldom sign the same petition
or join awkwardly the same shouting march,
neither of us, I hope, would leave through those doors
on the right or on the left marked HYGIENE.

Donald, you're such a northern-rooted man
                                    you've moved again.
Is home only home away from it? Still poets
jog eagerly, each molehill mistaken
for Parnassus – such energy articulate!
But where's the avant-garde when the procession
runs continuously in a closed circle?

So many open questions to one who prefers
                                    fugitive ways.
Of course I salute your gifted contradictions –
your two profiles almost the same – like Martin
    Guerre's.
I too am a reluctant puritan, feel uneasy
sometimes as if I travelled without ticket.
Yet here I am in England way out in the centre.

A sea-shell for Vernon Watkins

A stage moon and he, too, unreal, unearthed.
Then two shadows athletic down the cliffs
of Pennard near the nightshift of the sea.
He spoke of Yeats and Dylan, his sonorous
pin-ups. I thought, *relentless romantic!*
Darkness stayed in a cave and I lifted
a sea-shell from his shadow when he big-talked
how the dead resume the silence of God.

The bank calls in its debts and all are earthed.
Only one shadow at Pennard today
and listening to another sea-shell I found,
startled, its phantom sea utterly silent
– the shell's cochlea scooped out. Yet appropriate
that small void, that interruption of sound,
for what should be heard in a shell at Pennard
but the stopped breath of a poet who once sang loud?

Others gone also, like you dispensable,
famed names once writ in gold on spines of books
now rarely opened, the young asking, 'Who?'
The beaches of the world should be strewn with such
dumb shells while the immortal sea syllables
in self-love its own name, 'Sea, Sea, Sea, Sea.'
I turn to leave Pennard. This shell is useless.
If I could cry I would but not for you.

Imitations

In this house, in this afternoon room,
my son and I. The other side of glass
snowflakes whitewash the shed roof and the grass
this surprised April. My son is sixteen,
an approximate man. He is my chameleon,
my soft diamond, my deciduous evergreen.

Eyes half closed he listens to pop forgeries
of music – how hard it is to know – and perhaps
dreams of some school Juliet I don't know.
Meanwhile, beyond the bending window,
gusting suddenly, despite a sky half blue,
a blur of white blossom, whiter snow.

And I stare, oh immortal springtime, till
I'm elsewhere and the age my cool son is,
my father alive again (I, his duplicate),
his high breath, my low breath, sticking to the glass
while two white butterflies stumble, held each
to each as if by elastic, and pass.

One Sunday afternoon

In the courtyard my son with a football.
Here, a woodwormed room fit for suicide.
Locus suspectus. Oakbeams the hack described
where the squire swung two hundred years ago
to become, according to the guidebook,
transparent. Despite leaves falling outside
who can believe in ghosts? Especially in daylight!

So if something stood now against those curtains
to wear their exact design, and if somehow
the window opened slowly like a sign,
how I'd be shaken – wondering whether it
or the colours were being blown apart.
(As in a station, sitting in a carriage,
it seems we move when other trains depart.)

But listen – a small coincidence – a slam
from the hall (the curtains shook) and I am
less rational, more alone, since in my book
not seeing is believing. Hauntings?
Just the hustling wind and a far door bangs
and bangs. So who's unhinged? No snubbed ghost
    leaving,
no footfall creaks a plank but my own.

All eerie junketings, tall stories of
spooks grieving, the sounds of dread, can go hang
– and this room, too, quiet as language of the roses
or moss upon a wall. I hear nothing
when I hold my breath to hear it breathing.
Instead, from the courtyard, the bounce bounce
of a football and I feel comforted.

In my fashion

Dear, they said that woman resembled you.
Was that why I went with her, flirted with her,
raised my right hand to her left breast
till I heard the still sad music of humanity?
I complimented you! Why do you object?

Still you shrill, discover everything untrue:
your doppelgänger does not own your birthmarks,
cannot know our blurred nights together.
That music was cheap – a tune on a comb at best,
harsh and grating. Yes, you chasten me

and subdue. Well, that woman was contraband
and compared with you mere counterfeit.
Snow on the apple tree is not apple blossom –
all her colours wrong, approximate,
as in a reproduction of a masterpiece.

Last words

Splendidly, Shakespeare's heroes,
Shakespeare's heroines, once the spotlight's on,
enact every night, with such grace, their verbose deaths.
Then great plush curtains, then smiling resurrection
to applause – and never their good looks gone.

The last recorded words too
of real kings, real queens, all the famous dead,
are but pithy pretences, quotable fictions
composed by anonymous men decades later,
never with ready notebooks at the bed.

Most do not know who they are
when they die or where they are, country or town,
nor which hand on their brow. Some clapped-out actor may
imagine distant clapping, bow, but no real queen
will sigh, 'Give me my robe, put on my crown.'

Death scenes not life-enhancing,
death scenes not beautiful nor with breeding;
yet bravo Sydney Carton, bravo Duc de Chavost
who, euphoric beside the guillotine, turned down
the corner of the page he was reading.

And how would I wish to go?
Not as in opera – that would offend –
nor like a blue-eyed cowboy shot and short of words,
but finger-tapping still our private morse, '. . . love you,'
before the last flowers and flies descend.